EASY TOMATO SAUCE COOKBOOK

50 DELICIOUS TOMATO SAUCE RECIPES

By
Chef Maggie Chow
Copyright © by Saxonberg Associates

Published by
BookSumo, a division of Saxonberg Associates
http://www.booksumo.com/

INTRODUCTION

Welcome to *The Effortless Chef Series*! Thank you for taking the time to download the *Easy Tomato Sauce Cookbook*. Come take a journey with me into the delights of easy cooking. The point of this cookbook and all my cookbooks is to exemplify the effortless nature of cooking simply.

In this book we focus on Tomato Sauce. You will find that even though the recipes are simple, the taste of the dishes is quite amazing.

So will you join me in an adventure of simple cooking? If the answer is yes (and I hope it is) please consult the table of contents to find the dishes you are most interested in. Once you are ready jump right in and start cooking.

— Chef Maggie Chow

TABLE OF CONTENTS

ANY ISSUES? CONTACT ME

If you find that something important to you is missing from this book please contact me at maggie@booksumo.com.

I will try my best to re-publish a revised copy taking your feedback into consideration and let you know when the book has been revised with you in mind.

:)

— Chef Maggie Chow

LEGAL NOTES

COMMON ABBREVIATIONS

cup(s)	C.
tablespoon	tbsp
teaspoon	tsp
ounce	oz.
pound	lb

*All units used are standard American measurements

Chapter 1: Easy Tomato Sauce Recipes

Pasta in Italian Style

Ingredients

- 2 tbsp olive oil
- 1 onion, diced
- 1 clove garlic, minced
- 1 (14.5 oz.) can Italian-style diced tomatoes, undrained
- 1 tbsp dried basil leaves
- 3/4 tsp white sugar
- 1/4 tsp dried oregano
- 1/4 tsp salt
- 1/8 tsp ground black pepper
- 1/2 C. heavy cream
- 1 tbsp butter

Directions

- In a pan, heat the oil on medium heat and sauté the onion and garlic till tender. Add the remaining ingredients except the butter and heavy cream and bring to a boil.
- Boil for about 5 minutes. Remove everything from the heat and immediately, stir in the butter and heavy cream.
- Now, place the pan on low heat and simmer for about 5 minutes.

Amount per serving (5 total)

Timing Information:

Preparation	5 m
Cooking	15 m
Total Time	20 m

Nutritional Information:

Calories	182 kcal
Fat	16.6 g
Carbohydrates	6.7g
Protein	1.7 g
Cholesterol	39 mg
Sodium	270 mg

* Percent Daily Values are based on a 2,000 calorie diet.

VEGETARIAN-FRIENDLY MARINARA SAUCE

Ingredients

- 3 tbsp olive oil
- 1/2 onion, chopped
- 8 large tomatoes, peeled and cut into big chunks
- 6 cloves garlic, minced
- 1 bay leaf
- 1/2 C. red wine
- 1 tbsp honey
- 2 tsp dried basil
- 1 tsp oregano
- 1 tsp dried marjoram
- 1 tsp salt
- 1/2 tsp ground black pepper
- 1/4 tsp fennel seed
- 1/4 tsp crushed red pepper
- 2 tsp balsamic vinegar

Directions

- In a pan, heat the oil on medium heat and sauté the onion for about 5 minutes.
- Add the tomatoes, bay leaf and garlic and bring to a boil.
- Reduce the heat to medium-low and simmer for about 30 minutes.
- Stir in the remaining ingredients except vinegar and again bring to a gentle simmer.

- Simmer for about 30 minutes.
- Remove everything from the heat and immediately, stir in the vinegar.

Amount per serving (6 total)

Timing Information:

Preparation	15 m
Cooking	1 h 10 m
Total Time	1 h 25 m

Nutritional Information:

Calories	147 kcal
Fat	7.4 g
Carbohydrates	16.5g
Protein	2.7 g
Cholesterol	0 mg
Sodium	403 mg

* Percent Daily Values are based on a 2,000 calorie diet.

COMFORTING WEEKNIGHT DINNER

Ingredients

- 2 C. milk
- 2 C. chicken stock
- 1 C. yellow cornmeal
- 1 C. Parmesan cheese
- 2 C. spaghetti sauce

Directions

- Set your oven to 400 degrees F before doing anything else and grease a 9-inch square baking dish.
- In a large pan, add the broth and milk on medium-high heat and bring to a boil.
- Slowly, add the cornmeal, beating continuously.
- Reduce the heat to low and simmer for about 5 minutes, stirring continuously.
- Remove everything from the heat and immediately, stir in the Parmesan.
- Transfer the polenta into the prepared baking dish and top with the spaghetti sauce evenly.
- Cook everything in the oven for about 10 minutes.

Amount per serving (6 total)

Timing Information:

Preparation	5 m
Cooking	15 m
Total Time	20 m

Nutritional Information:

Calories	270 kcal
Fat	9 g
Carbohydrates	34.2g
Protein	12.2 g
Cholesterol	23 mg
Sodium	631 mg

* Percent Daily Values are based on a 2,000 calorie diet.

MEATY TOMATO SAUCE

Ingredients

- 1/4 C. olive oil
- 1 onion, finely diced
- 1 rib celery, finely diced
- 1 pinch salt
- 4 cloves garlic, minced
- 2 (28 oz.) cans whole peeled San Marzano tomatoes
- 2 tsp white sugar
- 1 tsp salt
- 1 tsp anchovy paste
- 1 tsp white wine vinegar
- 1/2 tsp dried Italian herbs
- 1 pinch red pepper flakes
- 1 tbsp tomato paste
- 2 tbsp chopped Italian flat-leaf parsley
- water, as needed

Directions

- In a large heavy pan, heat the oil on medium-low heat and sauté the celery, onion and a pinch of salt for about 15 minutes.
- Stir in the garlic and sauté for about 1 minute.
- Increase the heat to medium and stir in the vinegar, anchovy paste, sugar, herbs, red pepper flakes and salt.
- Cook till all the liquid is absorbed.

- Meanwhile in a large bowl, add the tomatoes with liquid and with your hands, crush them to a puree.
- Add the tomato paste in the pan and bring to a gentle simmer.
- Stir in the tomato puree and basil and again bring to a gentle simmer.
- Reduce the heat to low and simmer, stirring occasionally for about 1 1/2 hours, adding water if required.

Amount per serving (8 total)

Timing Information:

Preparation	15 m
Cooking	1 h 45 m
Total Time	2 h

Nutritional Information:

Calories	116 kcal
Fat	7.1 g
Carbohydrates	13g
Protein	2.2 g
Cholesterol	1 mg
Sodium	674 mg

* Percent Daily Values are based on a 2,000 calorie diet.

FRESHLY TASTING PASTA SAUCE

Ingredients

- 3 tbsp extra virgin olive oil
- 1 large onion, chopped
- 2 cloves garlic, crushed
- 2 (14.5 oz.) cans tomatoes, chopped
- 1/4 tsp red pepper flakes, or to taste
- 2 tsp balsamic vinegar
- 2 tsp white sugar
- 3/4 C. basil leaves, torn into pieces
- salt and ground black pepper to taste

Directions

- In a pan, heat the oil on medium heat and sauté the onion and garlic for about 5 minutes.
- Stir in the tomatoes, sugar, red pepper flakes and vinegar and bring to a boil.
- Reduce the heat to low and simmer, stirring occasionally for about 45-60 minutes.
- Remove everything from the heat and stir in the basil, salt and black pepper.

Amount per serving (4 total)

Timing Information:

Preparation	10 m
Cooking	50 m
Total Time	1 h

Nutritional Information:

Calories	155 kcal
Fat	10.5 g
Carbohydrates	14.9g
Protein	2.4 g
Cholesterol	0 mg
Sodium	293 mg

* Percent Daily Values are based on a 2,000 calorie diet.

PENNE WITH SUMMERTIME TOMATO SAUCE

Ingredients

- 2 C. cherry tomatoes
- 2 tbsp olive oil
- 2 cloves garlic, sliced
- salt and ground black pepper to taste
- 2 C. chicken broth
- 2 tbsp fresh oregano leaves
- 1/2 tsp red pepper flakes
- 14 oz. penne pasta
- 1/2 C. grated Parmigiano-Reggiano cheese

Directions

- In a pan, heat the oil on medium-low heat and cook the cherry tomatoes, garlic and salt for about 2-3 minutes.
- Stir in the broth and bring to a simmer.
- Simmer for about 10 minutes and stir in the red pepper flakes and oregano.
- With a stick blender, puree the tomato mixture till smooth.
- In a large pan of lightly salted boiling water, cook the penne for about 11 minutes, stirring occasionally.

- Drain the pasta completely and again place it in the pan on medium-low heat.
- Add the tomato sauce in the pan with the pasta and stir to combine.
- Cook everything for about 1-2 minutes.
- Stir in the cheese, salt and black pepper and remove everything from the heat.

Amount per serving (4 total)

Timing Information:

Preparation	15 m
Cooking	25 m
Total Time	40 m

Nutritional Information:

Calories	483 kcal
Fat	12.5 g
Carbohydrates	76.7g
Protein	18.2 g
Cholesterol	11 mg
Sodium	645 mg

* Percent Daily Values are based on a 2,000 calorie diet.

Tomato Sauce in Old-Family Style

Ingredients

- 35 fresh tomatoes, peeled, seeded and chopped
- 3 fresh hot chile peppers, seeded and chopped
- 4 red bell peppers, cored, seeded and cut into 2-inch pieces
- 1 large onion, chopped
- 2 C. apple cider vinegar
- 1/3 C. fresh lime juice
- 1 C. white sugar
- 1 C. packed brown sugar
- 1 tbsp salt, or amount to taste

Directions

- In a pan, add the tomatoes on medium heat and simmer for about 1 hour.
- Remove the excess liquid from the pan and stir in the remaining ingredients.
- Reduce the heat to low and simmer for about 3-5 hours.
- Remove everything from the heat and with a slotted spoon, remove the foam from the top.

- Transfer the sauce into hot sterilized jars, leaving about ¼ of an inch of space at the top.
- Tightly, cover everything with lids and heat in a boiling water bath for 10 mins.

Amount per serving (96 total)

Timing Information:

Preparation	35 m
Cooking	4 h
Total Time	4 h 35 m

Nutritional Information:

Calories	30 kcal
Fat	0.1 g
Carbohydrates	7.1g
Protein	0.6 g
Cholesterol	0 mg
Sodium	77 mg

* Percent Daily Values are based on a 2,000 calorie diet.

CLASSIC TOMATO SAUCE

Ingredients

- 2 tsp olive oil
- 1/2 C. minced onion
- 2 cloves garlic, crushed
- 1 (28 oz.) can crushed tomatoes
- 2 (6.5 oz.) cans canned tomato sauce
- 2 (6 oz.) cans tomato paste
- 1/2 C. water
- 2 tbsp white sugar
- 2 tbsp chopped fresh parsley
- 1 1/2 tsp dried basil
- 1 tbsp salt
- 1 tsp Italian seasoning
- 1/2 tsp fennel seeds
- 1/4 tsp ground black pepper

Directions

- In a large heavy pan, heat the oil on medium heat and sauté the onion and garlic for about 5-7 minutes.
- Add the remaining ingredients and stir to combine well, then bring to a simmer.
- Reduce the heat to low and simmer, stirring occasionally for about 60-90 minutes.

Amount per serving (10 total)

Timing Information:

Preparation	10 m
Cooking	1 h 5 m
Total Time	1 h 15 m

Nutritional Information:

Calories	86 kcal
Fat	1.4 g
Carbohydrates	17.9g
Protein	3.5 g
Cholesterol	0 mg
Sodium	1265 mg

* Percent Daily Values are based on a 2,000 calorie diet.

Refreshing Tomato Sauce for Lamb

Ingredients

- 2/3 C. extra-virgin olive oil
- 1/4 C. white wine vinegar
- 1 tsp salt
- freshly ground black pepper to taste
- 2 tsp Dijon mustard
- 1/2 tsp white sugar
- 1/3 C. chopped fresh mint
- 2 plum tomatoes, chopped

Directions

- In a large bowl, add all the ingredients except the tomatoes and mint and beat till well combined.
- Stir in the tomatoes and mint.

Amount per serving (6 total)

Timing Information:

Preparation	10 m
Cooking	10 m
Total Time	10 m

Nutritional Information:

Calories	237 kcal
Fat	25 g
Carbohydrates	2.8g
Protein	0.5 g
Cholesterol	0 mg
Sodium	433 mg

* Percent Daily Values are based on a 2,000 calorie diet.

5-Ingredient Tomato Sauce

Ingredients

- 1/4 C. low-sodium canned chicken broth
- 1/4 C. dry vermouth or dry white wine
- 4 canned tomatoes, chopped
- 1/2 tsp minced fresh rosemary
- 1 tbsp butter

Directions

- In a skillet, add all the ingredients except the butter and bring to a boil.
- Cook till the liquid reduces to half.
- Add the butter and immediately, stir till smooth.
- Serve immediately with the steak.

Amount per serving (4 total)

Timing Information:

Preparation	10m
Cooking	10m
Total Time	20m

Nutritional Information:

Calories	70 kcal
Fat	3.1 g
Carbohydrates	6.6g
Protein	1.1 g
Cholesterol	8 mg
Sodium	188 mg

* Percent Daily Values are based on a 2,000 calorie diet.

TRADITIONAL MEXICAN TOMATO SAUCE

Ingredients

- 1 clove garlic, peeled
- 5 serrano peppers
- 1/2 onion, cut into 4 wedges
- 10 roma tomatoes
- sea salt to taste

Directions

- With a large piece of foil, cover a large skillet and heat on medium-high heat.
- Add all the vegetables and roast the garlic for about 5 minutes, followed by 10 minutes for the onions and peppers and 15 minutes for the tomatoes.
- Remove everything from the skillet and keep it aside to cool completely.
- In a food processor, add the vegetables and salt and pulse till smooth.
- Transfer the sauce into the airtight jars and preserve in the refrigerator for about 1 week.

Amount per serving (10 total)

Timing Information:

Preparation	10 m
Cooking	15 m
Total Time	40 m

Nutritional Information:

Calories	17 kcal
Fat	0.2 g
Carbohydrates	3.8g
Protein	0.7 g
Cholesterol	0 mg
Sodium	36 mg

* Percent Daily Values are based on a 2,000 calorie diet.

GARDEN FRESH TOMATO SAUCE

Ingredients

- 10 ripe tomatoes
- 2 tbsp olive oil
- 2 tbsp butter
- 1 onion, chopped
- 1 green bell pepper, chopped
- 2 carrots, chopped
- 4 cloves garlic, minced
- 1/4 C. chopped fresh basil
- 1/4 tsp Italian seasoning
- 1/4 C. Burgundy wine
- 1 bay leaf 2 stalks celery
- 2 tbsp tomato paste

Directions

- In a large pan of boiling water, add the tomatoes and cook for about 1 minute.
- With a slotted spoon, transfer the tomatoes in a large bowl of chilled water.
- Keep it aside to cool and remove the peel and seeds.
- In a food processor, add 8 tomatoes and pulse till pureed.
- Chop the remaining tomatoes.

- In a large pan, heat the oil and butter on medium heat and sauté the garlic, bell pepper, onion and garlic for about 5 minutes.
- Stir in the chopped tomatoes, tomato puree and the remaining ingredients except the tomato paste and bring to a boil.
- Reduce the heat to low and simmer, covered for about 2 hours.
- Stir in the tomato paste and simmer for about 2 hours.
- Remove the celery and bay leaf before serving.

Amount per serving (6 total)

Timing Information:

Preparation	30 m
Cooking	4 h
Total Time	4 h 30 m

Nutritional Information:

Calories	149 kcal
Fat	8.9 g
Carbohydrates	15g
Protein	2.9 g
Cholesterol	10 mg
Sodium	105 mg

* Percent Daily Values are based on a 2,000 calorie diet.

TOMATO SAUCE IN ITALIAN STYLE

Ingredients

- 2 tbsp olive oil
- 1 onion, diced
- 1/4 C. chopped celery (optional)
- 1 small garlic clove, minced
- 1 lb. ground beef
- 40 oz. Italian-style stewed tomatoes
- 2 (6 oz.) cans tomato paste
- 1 (8 oz.) package sliced mushrooms, or to taste (optional)
- 1/2 C. grated Parmesan cheese, or to taste
- 1/4 C. parsley
- 1 1/2 tsp salt
- 1 tsp white sugar
- 1/4 tsp ground nutmeg
- 1/2 tsp dried oregano
- 1/8 tsp ground black pepper
- 1/4 tsp baking soda, or to taste

Directions

- In a large pan, heat the oil on medium-high heat and sauté the celery, onion and garlic for about 5 minutes.
- Add the beef and cook, stirring for about 5-7 minutes.

- Add the tomato paste and stewed tomatoes and stir till well combined and smooth.
- Stir in the remaining ingredients except the baking soda and cook, stirring occasionally for about 10 minutes.
- Stir in the baking soda and cook for about 10 minutes.

Amount per serving (10 total)

Timing Information:

Preparation	20 m
Cooking	30 m
Total Time	50 m

Nutritional Information:

Calories	201 kcal
Fat	9.6 g
Carbohydrates	17.6g
Protein	12.6 g
Cholesterol	32 mg
Sodium	980 mg

* Percent Daily Values are based on a 2,000 calorie diet.

FAMILY-FAVORITE MEAL

Ingredients

- 1 lb. ground beef
- 1 C. instant rice
- 1 white onion, chopped
- 1 egg
- 1 (28 oz.) can tomato sauce
- 28 fluid oz. water

Directions

- In a large bowl, add the beef, egg, onion and rice and mix till well combined.
- Make small sized balls from the mixture.
- In a large pan, add the tomato sauce and water and bring to a boil.
- Carefully, place the balls in the sauce and reduce the heat to medium-low.
- Simmer, covered for about 35 minutes.

Amount per serving (6 total)

Timing Information:

Preparation	10 m
Cooking	35 m
Total Time	45 m

Nutritional Information:

Calories	246 kcal
Fat	10.2 g
Carbohydrates	21.8g
Protein	16.8 g
Cholesterol	75 mg
Sodium	745 mg

* Percent Daily Values are based on a 2,000 calorie diet.

EGGPLANT WITH SIMPLE SAUCE

Ingredients

- 1 eggplant, peeled and cut into 1/4-inch slices
- salt to taste
- 2 eggs
- 2 tbsp milk
- 1/2 C. grated Parmesan cheese
- 1/2 C. wheat germ
- 2 C. tomato sauce
- 1 tsp cayenne pepper
- 1 C. shredded mozzarella cheese

Directions

- Set your oven to 400 degrees F before doing anything else.
- In a baking sheet, place the eggplant slices and sprinkle with salt.
- Keep it aside for about 10 minutes.
- With a paper towel, pat dry the eggplant slices.
- Meanwhile in a shallow dish, add the milk and eggs and beat well.
- In another shallow dish, mix together wheat germ and Parmesan.
- Dip the eggplant slices in the egg mixture and coat with the Parmesan mixture evenly.

- Arrange the eggplant slices in the baking sheet and cook everything in the oven for about 15-20 minutes.
- Meanwhile in a pan, add the tomato sauce and cayenne pepper on medium heat and cook till heated completely.
- Pour the sauce over the eggplant slices and serve.

Amount per serving (4 total)

Timing Information:

Preparation	15 m
Cooking	15 m
Total Time	40 m

Nutritional Information:

Calories	237 kcal
Fat	11.7 g
Carbohydrates	16g
Protein	19.1 g
Cholesterol	120 mg
Sodium	1010 mg

* Percent Daily Values are based on a 2,000 calorie diet.

Extremely Yummy Tomato Pesto

Ingredients

- 2 C. fresh basil leaves
- 5 sun-dried tomatoes, softened
- 3 cloves garlic, crushed
- 1/4 tsp salt
- 3 tbsp toasted pine nuts
- 1/4 C. olive oil

Directions

- In a blender, add all the ingredients except the oil and pulse till well combined.
- While the motor is running, slowly, add the oil and pulse till the desired texture.

Amount per serving (3 total)

Timing Information:

Preparation	30 m
Cooking	30 m
Total Time	60m

Nutritional Information:

Calories	227 kcal
Fat	22.7 g
Carbohydrates	4.8g
Protein	3.6 g
Cholesterol	0 mg
Sodium	266 mg

* Percent Daily Values are based on a 2,000 calorie diet.

EXQUISITE PIZZA SAUCE

Ingredients

- 2 tbsp olive oil
- 1 (28 oz.) can crushed tomatoes
- 2 leaves basil, chopped
- 3 cloves garlic, chopped
- 1 pinch salt and ground black pepper to taste
- 1 pinch grated Parmesan cheese

Directions

- In a pan, heat the oil on low heat and all the ingredients except the cheese and bring to a gentle simmer.
- Stir in the Parmesan and serve.

Amount per serving (4 total)

Timing Information:

Preparation	10 m
Cooking	10 m
Total Time	20 m

Nutritional Information:

Calories	127 kcal
Fat	7.4 g
Carbohydrates	15g
Protein	3.5 g
Cholesterol	1 mg
Sodium	263 mg

* Percent Daily Values are based on a 2,000 calorie diet.

SUPER TASTY TOMATO SAUCE

Ingredients

- 3 tbsp olive oil
- 1 onion, chopped
- 4 cloves garlic, minced
- 1 lb. lean ground beef
- 2 (29 oz.) cans tomato sauce
- 1 (14.5 oz.) can stewed tomatoes
- 1/2 lb. pepperoni sausage, sliced

- 1 green bell pepper, chopped
- 1 (4.5 oz.) can mushrooms, drained and chopped
- 1/4 tsp garlic salt
- 1/4 tsp salt
- 1/4 tsp ground black pepper
- 1/4 tsp onion powder
- 1/4 tsp dried oregano
- 1/4 tsp Italian seasoning

Directions

- In a pan, heat the oil on medium heat and sauté the onion and garlic till caramelized.
- Remove everything from the heat and keep it aside.

- Heat a skillet on medium heat and cook the beef till browned completely.
- Stir in the onion mixture and cook for about 3 minutes.
- In a large pan, add the stewed tomatoes and tomato sauce and bring to a boil.
- Reduce the heat and simmer for about 15 minutes.
- Stir in the cooked beef mixture, green peppers and pepperoni and simmer, covered for about 30 minutes.
- Stir in the remaining ingredients and simmer for about 10 minutes.

Amount per serving (6 total)

Timing Information:

Preparation	10 m
Cooking	45 m
Total Time	55 m

Nutritional Information:

Calories	549 kcal
Fat	39.8 g
Carbohydrates	23.3g
Protein	27.1 g
Cholesterol	96 mg
Sodium	2509 mg

* Percent Daily Values are based on a 2,000 calorie diet.

Deeply Flavored Tomato Sauce

Ingredients

- 1 tbsp olive oil
- 2 1/2 lb. beef brisket, cubed
- 1 tsp salt
- 1 quart chicken stock
- 1 bay leaf
- 1/4 tsp dried rosemary
- 1 pint cherry tomatoes
- 5 cloves garlic
- 3 1/2 C. tomato sauce
- 1/4 C. heavy cream
- 2 shallots, chopped
- 1 tbsp extra-virgin olive oil
- 2 tbsp tomato paste
- 1 lb. penne pasta
- finely grated Parmigiano-Reggiano (optional)

Directions

- Heat a Dutch oven and cook the beef brisket and salt on high heat till browned completely.
- Add the rosemary, bay leaf and broth and bring to a boil.
- In a blender, add the tomatoes, shallot, garlic and oil and pulse till smooth.
- Reduce the heat to low and add the tomato mixture in the pan with the beef.

- Stir to combine and bring to a gentle simmer.
- Simmer, covered for about 2 1/2 hours.
- Now, simmer, uncovered for about 1 hour.
- Stir in the cream and tomato sauce and simmer till desired doneness.
- Stir in the salt and black pepper and remove everything from the heat.

Amount per serving (8 total)

Timing Information:

Preparation	15 m
Cooking	4 h
Total Time	4 h 15 m

Nutritional Information:

Calories	572 kcal
Fat	29.1 g
Carbohydrates	53g
Protein	26.8 g
Cholesterol	73 mg
Sodium	1349 mg

* Percent Daily Values are based on a 2,000 calorie diet.

Classic Tomato Spaghetti

Ingredients

- 12 oz. spaghetti
- 1 lb. lean ground beef
- 1 tsp salt
- 3/4 tsp white sugar
- 1 tsp dried oregano
- 1/4 tsp ground black pepper
- 1/8 tsp garlic powder
- 2 tbsp dried minced onion
- 2 1/2 C. chopped tomatoes
- 1 1/3 (6 oz.) cans tomato paste
- 1 (4.5 oz.) can sliced mushrooms

Directions

- Heat a skillet and cook the beef on medium heat till browned completely and drain off the excess fat.
- In a large pan, add the beef and the remaining ingredients except pasta and simmer, stirring occasionally for about 2 hours.
- Cook the spaghetti according to the package's directions and drain well.
- Pour the sauce over the spaghetti and serve.

Amount per serving (5 total)

Timing Information:

Preparation	15m
Cooking	2 h
Total Time	2h 15m

Nutritional Information:

Calories	557 kcal
Fat	20.3 g
Carbohydrates	65.7g
Protein	28.2 g
Cholesterol	68 mg
Sodium	1002 mg

* Percent Daily Values are based on a 2,000 calorie diet.

LAVISH SAUSAGE DINNER

Ingredients

- 2 (1 lb.) packages smoked sausage, sliced
- 1 C. water
- 2 tbsp all-purpose flour
- 1 (14.5 oz.) can diced tomatoes
- 1 (8 oz.) can tomato sauce
- 1 cube beef bouillon
- 1 lb. fresh green beans, trimmed and snapped

Directions

- Heat a skillet on medium heat and cook the sausage for about 5 minutes.
- Meanwhile in a bowl, mix together the flour and water.
- Add the flour mixture to the skillet, stirring continuously.
- Stir in the remaining ingredients and simmer, stirring occasionally till the sauce becomes thick.

Amount per serving (8 total)

Timing Information:

Preparation	10 m
Cooking	20 m
Total Time	30 m

Nutritional Information:

Calories	485 kcal
Fat	36.2 g
Carbohydrates	11.2g
Protein	27.3 g
Cholesterol	77 mg
Sodium	2042 mg

* Percent Daily Values are based on a 2,000 calorie diet.

WONDERFULLY COLORFUL DINNER

Ingredients

- 1 tbsp olive oil
- 1 red bell pepper, seeded and cut into 1-2-inch long strips
- 1 zucchini, sliced thickly
- 1 small eggplant, sliced
- 1 large sweet onion, cut into 8 portions
- 3/4 C. frozen broad beans
- 1 (14.5 oz.) can diced tomatoes
- 2 tbsp balsamic vinegar
- 1 C. couscous
- 1 C. vegetable stock

Directions

- Set your grill on high heat and grease the grill grate with olive oil.
- Cook the bell pepper, eggplant, zucchini and onion on the grill for about 15 minutes, flipping occasionally.
- Transfer the vegetables into a pan with the remaining ingredients and simmer for a few minutes.
- Meanwhile in a heatproof bowl, add the couscous with the boiling broth and stir to combine.

- Keep it aside for about 2-3 minutes, stirring occasionally.
- Transfer the couscous to serving plates and top with the vegetable mixture.

Amount per serving (4 total)

Timing Information:

Preparation	20 m
Cooking	15 m
Total Time	35 m

Nutritional Information:

Calories	317 kcal
Fat	4.5 g
Carbohydrates	59.2g
Protein	10.7 g
Cholesterol	0 mg
Sodium	326 mg

* Percent Daily Values are based on a 2,000 calorie diet.

SIMPLY DELICIOUS TOMATO SAUCE

Ingredients

- 2 tbsp olive oil
- 7 cloves garlic, minced
- 1 (6 oz.) can tomato paste
- 1 (28 oz.) can crushed tomatoes
- 2 (28 oz.) cans tomato puree
- 1/2 tsp ground black pepper
- 1/2 tsp salt
- 2 tsp dried basil leaves
- 1 tsp white sugar

Directions

- In a large pan, heat the oil and sauté the garlic till aromatic and reduce the heat to low.
- Stir in the tomato paste and simmer for about 5 minutes.
- Stir in the remaining ingredients and simmer for about 3 hours.

Amount per serving (14 total)

Timing Information:

Preparation	10 m
Cooking	3 h
Total Time	3 h 10 m

Nutritional Information:

Calories	91 kcal
Fat	2.4 g
Carbohydrates	17.3g
Protein	3.4 g
Cholesterol	0 mg
Sodium	700 mg

* Percent Daily Values are based on a 2,000 calorie diet.

EASIEST TOMATO SAUCE

Ingredients

- 1 lb. cherry tomatoes
- 1 red onion, finely chopped
- 1 tbsp balsamic vinegar
- 1 tsp chopped fresh red chile pepper
- 1 tsp crushed garlic
- 1 pinch Italian seasoning
- 1 tsp white sugar
- salt and pepper to taste

Directions

- In a pan, mix together all the ingredients on medium-low heat and simmer for about 15 minutes.
- With the back of a spoon, crush the tomatoes completely.
- Cook, stirring occasionally, for about 45 minutes.

Amount per serving (12 total)

Timing Information:

Preparation	15 m
Cooking	1 h
Total Time	1 h 15 m

Nutritional Information:

Calories	14 kcal
Fat	0.1 g
Carbohydrates	3.3g
Protein	0.5 g
Cholesterol	0 mg
Sodium	4 mg

* Percent Daily Values are based on a 2,000 calorie diet.

Italian Tomato Sauce with Lobster

Ingredients

- 1/4 C. olive oil
- 1 onion, chopped
- 1 small garlic clove, crushed
- 1 tbsp chopped fresh parsley
- 6 (6 oz.) lobster tails, thawed
- 1 (28 oz.) can crushed tomatoes
- 1 (8 oz.) can tomato sauce
- 3 tbsp chopped fresh basil
- salt and ground black pepper to taste

Directions

- In a pan, heat the oil on medium heat and sauté the onion and garlic for about 8 minutes.
- Stir in the lobster tails and parsley and cook for about 10-15 minutes.
- Stir in the remaining ingredients and reduce the heat to low.
- Simmer, stirring occasionally for about 1 hour.

- Remove the lobster tails from the sauce and shake off the excess sauce.
- Serve the lobster tails with the sauce.

Amount per serving (6 total)

Timing Information:

Preparation	20 m
Cooking	1 h 15 m
Total Time	1 h 35 m

Nutritional Information:

Calories	295 kcal
Fat	13.7 g
Carbohydrates	15.1g
Protein	29.3 g
Cholesterol	101 mg
Sodium	891 mg

* Percent Daily Values are based on a 2,000 calorie diet.

ARGENTINIAN CHICKEN IN TOMATO SAUCE

Ingredients

- 8 bone-in chicken breast halves, with skin
- 1 C. all-purpose flour
- 1 tbsp vegetable oil
- 2 (15 oz.) cans tomato sauce
- 2 (15 oz.) cans whole kernel corn
- 1/2 C. diced onion
- 2 cloves garlic, minced
- 2 tbsp chili powder
- 1/2 tsp crushed red pepper flakes
- salt to taste

Directions

- Roll the chicken breast halves in the flour evenly.
- In a large skillet, heat the oil and cook the chicken for about 5-7 minutes.
- Remove everything from the heat and keep it aside.
- In a pan, mix together the onion, corn and tomato sauce and bring to a boil.

- Stir in the chicken and the remaining ingredients and reduce the heat to low.
- Simmer for about 1 hour.

Amount per serving (8 total)

Timing Information:

Preparation	30 m
Cooking	1 h
Total Time	1 h 30 m

Nutritional Information:

Calories	476 kcal
Fat	10.5 g
Carbohydrates	40.5g
Protein	56.6 g
Cholesterol	137 mg
Sodium	1003 mg

* Percent Daily Values are based on a 2,000 calorie diet.

Awesome Zucchini with Tomato Sauce

Ingredients

- 2 tbsp olive oil
- 4 zucchini - peeled, sliced lengthwise, and sliced
- 2 tsp dried oregano
- 2 tsp dried basil
- 1 1/2 C. tomato sauce
- 1/4 C. Parmesan cheese

Directions

- In a large skillet, heat the oil on medium-high heat and sauté the zucchini for about 5-10 minutes.
- Stir in the tomato sauce and herbs and cook for about 5 minutes.
- Serve with a topping of Parmesan.

Amount per serving (4 total)

Timing Information:

Preparation	10 m
Cooking	10 m
Total Time	20 m

Nutritional Information:

Calories	126 kcal
Fat	8.6 g
Carbohydrates	9.8g
Protein	4.8 g
Cholesterol	4 mg
Sodium	570 mg

* Percent Daily Values are based on a 2,000 calorie diet.

SUPER-HEALTH TOMATO SAUCE

Ingredients

- 4 large tomatoes
- 2 large red bell peppers, seeded and diced
- 1 onion, coarsely chopped
- 1 tsp minced garlic
- salt and pepper to taste

Directions

- In a pan of boiling water, cook the tomatoes till the skin starts to split.
- Drain well and rinse under cold water to cool.
- Remove the peel of the tomatoes and place them in a large skillet on low heat.
- With a potato masher, mash the tomatoes completely.
- Stir in the onion, bell pepper and garlic and simmer for about 20 minutes.
- Stir in the salt and black pepper and remove everything from the heat.

Amount per serving (6 total)

Timing Information:

Preparation	5 m
Cooking	30 m
Total Time	35 m

Nutritional Information:

Calories	47 kcal
Fat	0.4 g
Carbohydrates	9.9g
Protein	1.8 g
Cholesterol	0 mg
Sodium	9 mg

* Percent Daily Values are based on a 2,000 calorie diet.

STEWED TOMATOES ASIAN STYLE

Ingredients

- 12 roma tomatoes - peeled, quartered, and seeded
- 1/4 onion, minced
- 1/3 C. water
- 1/2 tsp mustard seed
- 1/3 tsp dry mustard powder
- 1 large clove garlic, minced
- 1 bay leaf
- 1/8 tsp ground black pepper
- 1/2 tsp soy sauce
- salt to taste

Directions

- In a heavy pan, mix together all the ingredients except the soy sauce and salt on medium heat.
- Bring everything to a gentle boil and simmer for about 10 minutes.
- Stir in the soy sauce and simmer for about 5 minutes.
- Stir in the salt and remove everything from the heat.
- Discard the bay leaf before serving.

Amount per serving (4 total)

Timing Information:

Preparation	15 m
Cooking	15 m
Total Time	30 m

Nutritional Information:

Calories	45 kcal
Fat	0.6 g
Carbohydrates	9.4g
Protein	2.1 g
Cholesterol	0 mg
Sodium	48 mg

* Percent Daily Values are based on a 2,000 calorie diet.

Marvelous Shrimp Tomato Sauce

Ingredients

- 2 lb. medium shrimp - peeled and deveined
- 4 cloves garlic, peeled and minced
- 2 tbsp olive oil
- 8 plum tomatoes, finely chopped
- salt
- cayenne pepper
- 1 tbsp butter

Directions

- In a large skillet, heat the oil on medium heat and sauté the garlic for about 2 minutes.
- Stir in the tomatoes, salt and cayenne pepper and bring to a boil.
- Simmer for about 15 minutes, stirring occasionally.
- Sprinkle the shrimp with the salt and add everything to the pan.
- Simmer for about 3-5 minutes.
- Stir in the butter and remove everything from the heat.

Amount per serving (4 total)

Timing Information:

Preparation	20 m
Cooking	20 m
Total Time	40 m

Nutritional Information:

Calories	288 kcal
Fat	11.8 g
Carbohydrates	6g
Protein	38.4 g
Cholesterol	353 mg
Sodium	11006 mg

* Percent Daily Values are based on a 2,000 calorie diet.

MILANESE STYLE TOMATO SAUCE

Ingredients

- 4 lb. roma tomatoes, chopped
- 1 C. butter, cubed
- 6 cloves garlic, chopped
- 1/4 C. chopped fresh thyme
- 2 tbsp cracked black pepper
- 2 tbsp kosher salt

Directions

- Set your oven to 350 degrees F before doing anything else and line a baking sheet with parchment paper.
- In a bowl, add all the ingredients except the salt and black pepper and toss to coat well.
- Transfer the tomato mixture onto the prepared baking sheet and cook everything in the oven for about 1 hour.
- Remove everything from the oven and keep it aside to cool slightly.
- In a blender, add the tomato mixture, salt and black pepper and pulse till smooth.

Amount per serving (16 total)

Timing Information:

Preparation	10 m
Cooking	1 h
Total Time	1 h 10 m

Nutritional Information:

Calories	126 kcal
Fat	11.8 g
Carbohydrates	5.5g
Protein	1.3 g
Cholesterol	31 mg
Sodium	808 mg

* Percent Daily Values are based on a 2,000 calorie diet.

EGGS PERSIAN STYLE

Ingredients

- 1 1/2 tbsp olive oil
- 1 small onion, finely chopped
- 1 garlic clove, finely chopped
- 4 -5 medium tomatoes, peeled, seeded and chopped
- salt (to taste)
- pepper (to taste)
- 4 eggs
- 1 tbsp chives, finely chopped

Directions

- In a nonstick skillet, heat the oil on medium-high heat and sauté the onion and garlic for about 1 minute.
- Reduce the heat to medium and sauté for about 3-4 minutes.
- Stir in the tomatoes and simmer for about 10 minutes, then stir in the salt and black pepper.
- With a spoon, make 4 wells in the tomato mixture.

- Carefully break 1 egg in each well and cook, covered partially till desired doneness.
- Carefully, transfer 1 egg with some sauce in each serving plate.
- Serve with a garnishing of the chives.

Amount per serving: 2

Timing Information:

Preparation	10 mins
Total Time	30 mins

Nutritional Information:

Calories	293.4
Fat	20.1g
Cholesterol	372.0mg
Sodium	1156.2mg
Carbohydrates	14.1g
Protein	15.2g

* Percent Daily Values are based on a 2,000 calorie diet.

Smoky Tomato Sauce

Ingredients

- 2 lb. large tomatoes, halved
- 4 garlic cloves, minced
- 1 tsp dried Italian herb seasoning
- 1/2 tsp sugar
- 1 tsp salt
- 1/2 tsp black pepper
- 2 tbsp olive oil

Directions

- Set your oven to 400 degrees F before doing anything else and grease a large baking sheet with the olive oil.
- Spread the olives in the prepared baking sheet, followed by the garlic, herbs, sugar, salt and black pepper.
- Arrange the tomatoes over the olives mixture, cut side down and cook everything in the oven for about 30-40 minutes.
- Remove everything from the heat and let it cool slightly.
- Discard the skin of the tomatoes and with a fork, break up the flesh completely.
- Serve warm.

Amount per serving: 4

Timing Information:

Preparation	20 mins
Total Time	2 hrs 20 mins

Nutritional Information:

Calories	107.7
Fat	7.2g
Cholesterol	0.0mg
Sodium	593.4mg
Carbohydrates	10.5g
Protein	2.2g

* Percent Daily Values are based on a 2,000 calorie diet.

Rice With Tomato Sauce Spanish Style

Ingredients

- 1 1/2 C. rice
- 2 C. chicken broth
- 1 C. tomato sauce
- 3 minced garlic cloves
- 1/4 C. chopped onion
- 2 tbsp oil

Directions

- In a pan, heat the oil on medium heat and sauté the onion and garlic for about 1-2 minutes.
- Stir in the rice and cook everything for about 5 minutes.
- Slowly, stir in the tomato sauce and broth and bring to a boil.
- Reduce the heat to low and simmer, covered for about 20 minutes.

Amount per serving: 4

Timing Information:

Preparation	10 mins
Total Time	30 mins

Nutritional Information:

Calories	364.9
Fat	8.0g
Cholesterol	0.0mg
Sodium	695.7mg
Carbohydrates	63.4g
Protein	8.3g

* Percent Daily Values are based on a 2,000 calorie diet.

CHICKPEAS IN TOMATO SAUCE

Ingredients

- 1 tbsp vegetable oil
- 1 onion, large, finely chopped
- 4 garlic cloves, minced
- 2 tbsp minced gingerroot
- 1 tsp ground cumin
- 1 tsp salt
- 1/2 tsp black pepper
- 2 tsp balsamic vinegar
- 2 (14 oz.) cans diced tomatoes
- 2 (15 oz.) cans chickpeas, rinsed and drained
- chopped green onion

Directions

- In a large pan, heat the oil on medium heat and sauté the onion for about 10 minutes. Stir in the ginger, garlic, cumin, salt and black pepper and sauté for about 1 minute.
- Stir in the tomatoes and vinegar and bring to a boil on medium-high heat.
- Add the chickpeas and reduce the heat to low.
- Simmer, covered for about 45 minutes, stirring occasionally.
- Serve with a garnishing of green onion.

Amount per serving: 6

Timing Information:

Preparation	15 mins
Total Time	1 hr 15 mins

Nutritional Information:

Calories	227.8
Fat	4.2g
Cholesterol	0.0mg
Sodium	820.4mg
Carbohydrates	40.5g
Protein	8.6g

* Percent Daily Values are based on a 2,000 calorie diet.

AUTHENTIC TOMATO SAUCE

Ingredients

- 2 tbsp olive oil
- 6 garlic cloves (minced)
- 2 tsp chili flakes
- 1 (28 oz.) cans crushed tomatoes
- 1/2 C. water
- 1/4 C. fresh basil (chopped)
- 1 tsp salt

Directions

- In a frying pan, cook the oil, chili flakes and garlic on medium-high heat till just aromatic.
- Stir in the tomatoes, 1/2 of the basil and salt and bring to a boil.
- Add the water and reduce the heat, then simmer for about 1 hour.
- Serve with a garnishing of the remaining basil alongside the pasta of your choice.

Amount per serving: 4

Timing Information:

Preparation	10 mins
Total Time	1 hr 40 mins

Nutritional Information:

Calories	122.1
Fat	7.3g
Cholesterol	0.0mg
Sodium	1021.4mg
Carbohydrates	14.6g
Protein	2.0g

* Percent Daily Values are based on a 2,000 calorie diet.

Superb Tuna Tomato Sauce

Ingredients

- 2 -3 tbsp olive oil
- 1 medium onion, chopped
- 2 garlic cloves, chopped
- 1 C. canned tomato with juice
- 1/4 tsp dried oregano
- salt & freshly ground black pepper
- 1 (6 1/2 oz.) cans tuna, drained, flaked
- 2 tbsp sliced green olives, with some juice
- 1 tbsp capers, with some juice
- 8 oz. spaghetti
- grated parmesan cheese

Directions

- In a heavy pan, heat the oil and sauté the onion and garlic till tender.
- Add the tomatoes, oregano, salt and black pepper.
- Reduce the heat to low.
- Simmer for about 10 minutes.
- Stir in the olives, tuna and capers and simmer till the sauce becomes thick.

- Meanwhile in a large pan of lightly salted boiling water, cook the pasta till just tender for about 9 mins.
- Drain well and add in the pan of sauce and gently stir to combine.
- Serve with a garnishing of cheese.

Amount per serving: 2

Timing Information:

Preparation	5 mins
Total Time	25 mins

Nutritional Information:

Calories	735.2
Fat	21.2g
Cholesterol	34.9mg
Sodium	475.5mg
Carbohydrates	96.6g
Protein	38.2g

* Percent Daily Values are based on a 2,000 calorie diet.

HARVEST TIME TOMATO SAUCE

Ingredients

- 1/2 bushel fresh tomato
- 2 garlic cloves, chopped
- 4 medium onions, chopped
- 2 tbsp oil
- 3 (15 oz.) cans tomato paste
- 1 1/2 C. sugar
- 1/2 C. salt
- 2 tbsp oregano
- 2 tbsp Italian seasoning mix
- 1 (5 oz.) packages spaghetti sauce mix

Directions

- Cut the tomatoes and pulse in a food processor and in a food mill.
- Transfer the tomatoes into a pan. In another pan, heat the oil and sauté the onion and garlic till tender. Remove everything from the heat and keep it aside to cool. Process the onion mixture through the food mill and transfer into the pan with the tomatoes.
- Add the remaining ingredients and bring to a gentle simmer.
- Boil, stirring occasionally for about 2 hours.
- Transfer the sauce into hot sterilized jars and process into a water bath for about 40 minutes.

Amount per serving: 10

Timing Information:

Preparation	1 hr
Total Time	3 hrs

Nutritional Information:

Calories	264.6
Fat	0.0mg
Cholesterol	6676.6mg
Sodium	2g
Carbohydrates	58.7g
Protein	6.1g

* Percent Daily Values are based on a 2,000 calorie diet.

VIBRANT TASTING TOMATO SAUCE

Ingredients

- 2 onions, medium, chopped
- 2 garlic cloves, crushed
- 1/4 C. vegetable oil
- 2 C. tomatoes, large, peeled, seeded and chopped
- 1/3 C. brown sugar
- 1/4 C. white vinegar
- 1 tsp Worcestershire sauce
- 1 tsp celery seed
- 1/2 tsp salt
- 1/4 tsp dry mustard
- 2 green peppers, chopped
- 1/2 tsp pepper

Directions

- In a pan, heat the oil and sauté the onion and garlic till tender.
- Stir in the remaining ingredients except the green peppers and bring to a boil.
- Cook, stirring occasionally for about 30 minutes.
- Stir in the peppers and cook till desired thickness.

Amount per serving: 4

Timing Information:

Preparation	15 mins
Total Time	55 mins

Nutritional Information:

Calories	249.9
Fat	14.1g
Cholesterol	0.0mg
Sodium	320.0mg
Carbohydrates	30.7g
Protein	2.1g

* Percent Daily Values are based on a 2,000 calorie diet.

MOUTH WATERING TOMATO SAUCE

Ingredients

- 2 tbsp olive oil
- 1 garlic clove, finely chopped
- 1/2 C. fresh parsley, chopped
- 1/2 tsp salt
- 1/2 tsp fresh black pepper
- 2 C. cherry tomatoes, halved
- 1/2 tsp lemon zest, grated
- 1/4 tsp sugar
- 2 tbsp fresh lemon juice

Directions

- In a skillet, heat the oil on medium-low heat and sauté the half of the parsley, garlic, salt and black pepper for about 2 minutes.
- Increase the heat to medium-high and stir in the lemon zest, tomatoes and sugar.
- Cook, stirring continuously for about 2 minutes.
- Stir in the remaining parsley and lemon juice and remove everything from the heat.

Amount per serving: 4

Timing Information:

Preparation	10 mins
Total Time	14 mins

Nutritional Information:

Calories	80.3
Fat	6.9g
Cholesterol	0.0mg
Sodium	299.0mg
Carbohydrates	4.6g
Protein	0.9g

* Percent Daily Values are based on a 2,000 calorie diet.

YUMMY PIZZA SAUCE

Ingredients

- 2 (28 oz.) cans whole Italian-style peeled tomatoes
- 1 tbsp dried oregano
- 1 tsp kosher salt
- 2 garlic cloves, minced
- 8 large fresh basil leaves, coarsely chopped
- 1/2 tsp red pepper flakes

Directions

- In a large pan, add the tomatoes with liquid on medium-low heat and with the back of a spoon, crush them.
- Stir in the salt and oregano and simmer for about 50 minutes.
- Remove everything from the heat and keep it aside to cool.
- Stir in the basil, garlic and red pepper flakes and serve immediately.

Amount per serving: 8

Timing Information:

Preparation	10 mins
Total Time	1 hr

Nutritional Information:

Calories	36.4
Fat	0.3g
Cholesterol	0.0mg
Sodium	474.2mg
Carbohydrates	8.3g
Protein	1.7g

* Percent Daily Values are based on a 2,000 calorie diet.

Parisian Style Fish in Tomato Sauce

Ingredients

- 1 onion, peeled and chopped
- oil
- 14 oz. tomatoes, chopped
- 1/2 C. dry white wine
- 2 tbsp parsley, finely chopped
- 1/2 tsp black pepper, coarsely ground
- 1 tsp sugar
- 1 tsp salt
- 2 lb. fish fillets, any kind
- 1 C. fresh cream

Directions

- In a pan, heat the oil on medium heat and sauté the onion till tender.
- Stir in the tomatoes, parsley, sugar, salt, black pepper and wine and bring to a boil.
- Stir in the fish fillets and simmer for about 7 minutes.
- With a slotted spoon, transfer the fish to a serving plate.
- Cover everything with foil to keep warm.
- Again boil the sauce till it reduces by half.

- Stir in the cream and cook everything with high heat till the desired thickness.
- Place the sauce over the fish and serve.

Amount per serving: 4

Timing Information:

Preparation	10 mins
Total Time	40 mins

Nutritional Information:

Calories	501.8
Fat	24.2g
Cholesterol	206.1mg
Sodium	789.4mg
Carbohydrates	10.2g
Protein	54.2g1

* Percent Daily Values are based on a 2,000 calorie diet.

Tomato Sauce in Traditional Mexican Style

Ingredients

- 2 (16 oz.) cans tomatoes
- 2 tbsp oil
- 1 C. onion, finely chopped
- 1 small jalapeno pepper, minced
- 2 garlic cloves, minced
- 2 tbsp red wine
- 1 tsp dried oregano
- 1 tsp dried ancho chile powder
- 1/2 tsp cumin
- 1/2 tsp dried basil

Directions

- Drain the tomatoes, reserving the liquid, then chop the tomatoes.
- In a pan, heat the oil on medium heat and sauté the onion, garlic and jalapeño for about 5 minutes.
- Add the tomatoes, reserved liquid, and the remaining ingredients and simmer for about 20-30 minutes, stirring occasionally.
- With a stick blender, puree the mixture completely.

Amount per serving: 6

Timing Information:

Preparation	10 mins
Total Time	50 mins

Nutritional Information:

Calories	86.9
Fat	4.9g
Cholesterol	0.0mg
Sodium	16.8mg
Carbohydrates	9.4g
Protein	1.8g

* Percent Daily Values are based on a 2,000 calorie diet.

FRENCH TOMATO SAUCE

Ingredients

- 3 tbsp unsalted butter
- 1/2 small onion, thinly sliced
- 3 mushrooms, thinly sliced
- 2 shallots, thinly sliced
- 1 small leek, white part, thinly sliced
- 1/4 tsp salt
- 1 tbsp brandy
- 1/4 C. madeira wine, plus
- 1 tbsp madeira wine
- 3 tomatoes, chopped
- 1 C. chicken broth
- 2 sprigs thyme
- 1 bay leaf
- 1/2 tsp salt
- 1/2 tsp black pepper

Directions

- In a skillet, melt 2 tbsp of the butter on medium heat and sauté the onion, leeks, shallots, mushrooms and salt for about 7 minutes.
- Stir in the 1/4 C. of the Madeira and brandy and increase the heat to high.
- Carefully, ignite the alcohol with a bbq lighter and cook till the flames vanish.

- Reduce the heat to medium-high and cook everything until the liquid reduces by half.
- Stir in the tomatoes, bay leaf, thyme and chicken broth and reduce the heat to low.
- Simmer for about 20 minutes.
- Remove everything from the heat and keep it aside to cool slightly.
- In a food processor, add the mixture and pulse till smooth.
- Return the sauce to the pan and stir in the remaining Madeira, remaining butter, salt and black pepper.

Amount per serving: 4

Timing Information:

Preparation	10 mins
Total Time	30 mins

Nutritional Information:

Calories	156.2
Fat	9.3g
Cholesterol	22.9mg
Sodium	636.1mg
Carbohydrates	10.6g
Protein	3.2g

* Percent Daily Values are based on a 2,000 calorie diet.

ENRICHING TOMATO SAUCE

Ingredients

- 1 lb ground beef
- 1 onion, chopped
- 2 cloves garlic, minced
- 1 (28 oz.) cans diced tomatoes
- 1/2 tsp dried oregano
- 1/2 tsp dried basil
- 1/2 tsp dried parsley
- 1/2 tsp white sugar
- salt and pepper, to taste
- 3/4 C. heavy cream
- 1 lb vermicelli, cooked and drained
- fresh grated parmesan cheese

Directions

- In a pan, heat the oil on medium heat and sear the beef and onion till browned. Stir in the tomatoes, sugar, dried herbs, salt and black pepper and bring to a boil.
- Reduce the heat to low and simmer for about 15 minutes.
- Stir in the cream and simmer till heated completely.
- Place the sauce over the pasta and serve with a garnishing of cheese.

Amount per serving: 4

Timing Information:

Preparation	10 mins
Total Time	30 mins

Nutritional Information:

Calories	870.1
Fat	35.6g
Cholesterol	138.2mg
Sodium	110.2mg
Carbohydrates	97.3g
Protein	38.9g

* Percent Daily Values are based on a 2,000 calorie diet.

TOMATO SAUCE IN GREEK STYLE

Ingredients

- 3 tbsp olive oil
- 1 onion, chopped fine
- 1 garlic clove, chopped fine
- 4 1/2 C. chopped tomatoes
- 2 tbsp chopped fresh parsley
- 2 tsp oregano
- 1 C. dry red wine
- 8 oz. tomato sauce
- 1/4 tsp ground cinnamon
- 1 pinch ground allspice
- fresh ground black pepper, to taste
- salt, to taste

Directions

- In a pan, heat the oil on medium heat and sauté the onion and garlic till tender.
- Stir in the tomatoes and herbs and simmer, covered for about 25 minutes.
- Stir in the remaining ingredients and simmer for about 20 more minutes.

Amount per serving: 1

Timing Information:

Preparation	15 mins
Total Time	1 hr

Nutritional Information:

Calories	135.5
Fat	7.1g
Cholesterol	0.0mg
Sodium	209.6mg
Carbohydrates	10.4g
Protein	2.0g

* Percent Daily Values are based on a 2,000 calorie diet.

Enjoyable Broccoli with Tomato Sauce

Ingredients

- 4 oz. pasta (Fusili works best!)
- 1/2 C. broccoli floret
- 2 -2 1/2 C. water

FOR THE SAUCE

- 3 medium tomatoes, finely chopped
- 1/2 medium onion, finely chopped
- 1/2 tsp dried basil
- 1/2 tsp oregano
- 1/2 tsp dried parsley
- 1 1/2 tsp olive oil
- salt
- pepper
- parmesan cheese, grated (optional)

Directions

- In a large pan of lightly salted boiling water, cook the pasta for about 5-8 minutes.
- Stir in the broccoli and cook for about 5-8 minutes.
- Drain well, reserving about 1/2 C of the cooking liquid.
- In a pan, heat the oil and sauté the onion till tender.

- Stir in the tomatoes, reserved cooking liquid, salt and black pepper.
- Simmer, covered for about 5 minutes.
- Increase the heat to high and cook, uncovered for about 5 minutes.
- Remove everything from the heat and immediately, stir in the pasta mixture and herbs.
- Serve hot with a topping of Parmesan.

Amount per serving: 2

Timing Information:

| Preparation | 5 mins |
| Total Time | 25 mins |

Nutritional Information:

Calories	291.4
Fat	4.7g
Cholesterol	0.0mg
Sodium	26.4mg
Carbohydrates	53.4g
Protein	9.9g

* Percent Daily Values are based on a 2,000 calorie diet.

MEATBALLS WITH TOMATO SAUCE MOROCCAN STYLE

Ingredients

- 1 1/4 lb. ground lamb
- 3 tsp paprika, divided
- 2 tsp cumin, divided
- 12 sprigs fresh parsley, leaves chopped and divided
- salt
- 1 large garlic clove, peeled and chopped
- 1 (15 oz.) cans diced tomatoes with juice, drained
- 1/4 C. olive oil
- 3 tbsp tomato paste
- 1 small onion, peeled and roughly chopped into 8 pieces

Directions

- For the meatballs, in a large bowl, add the lamb, 1/2 of parsley, 1 tsp of the cumin, 1 ½ tsp of the paprika and 1 tsp of the salt and mix till well combined.
- Make 1-inch balls from the mixture.

- In a food processor, add the tomatoes, onion, garlic, tomato paste, olive oil, remaining parsley and remaining spices and pulse till smooth.
- Transfer the mixture into a large skillet on medium heat and bring to a boil.
- Simmer for about 2-4 minutes and remove everything from the heat.
- Carefully, place the meatballs in the sauce and swirl the skillet to coat the meatballs with the sauce.
- Cook everything on medium heat for about 10-12 minutes.

Amount per serving: 4

Timing Information:

Preparation	0 mins
Total Time	45 mins

Nutritional Information:

Calories	565.9
Fat	47.4g
Cholesterol	103.6mg
Sodium	336.6mg
Carbohydrates	10.0g
Protein	25.6g

* Percent Daily Values are based on a 2,000 calorie diet.

POTATOES WITH TOMATO SAUCE IN SPANISH STYLE

Ingredients

Spicy Tomato Sauce

- 1 tbsp olive oil
- 1 C. chopped onion
- 2 garlic cloves, minced
- 1 (14 1/2 oz.) cans diced tomatoes
- 1/2 tsp crushed red pepper flakes

Potatoes

- 1/4 C. olive oil
- 1 lb red potatoes, peeled and cut into 1-inch cubes
- sea salt

Directions

- Set your oven to 400 degrees F before doing anything else.
- For the sauce, in a pan, heat the oil on medium heat and sauté the onion for about 10 minutes.
- Add the red pepper and tomatoes and simmer, covered for about 20 minutes.

- Remove everything from the heat and let it cool slightly.
- In a blender, add the tomato mixture and pulse till smooth, then transfer into a bowl.
- For the potatoes, in a skillet, heat the oil on medium heat and cook the potatoes till they are golden brown, stirring occasionally.
- Transfer the potato cubes onto a paper towel lined plate to drain.
- Now, place the potato cubes onto a baking sheet and cook everything in the oven for about 10 minutes.
- Serve immediately with a sprinkling of salt alongside the tomato sauce.

Amount per serving: 1

Timing Information:

Preparation	15 mins
Total Time	55 mins

Nutritional Information:

Calories	184.6
Fat	11.5g
Cholesterol	0.0mg
Sodium	154.4mg
Carbohydrates	19.4g
Protein	2.2g

* Percent Daily Values are based on a 2,000 calorie diet.

Moroccan Fava Beans in Tomato Sauce

Ingredients

- 2 (19 oz.) cans fava beans
- 3 tbsp olive oil
- 3 large onions, chopped
- 5 cloves garlic, minced
- 2 tbsp hot red pepper flakes
- 1/4 C. tomato sauce
- 3/4 C. hot water
- 3 tbsp fresh parsley, chopped
- salt & pepper
- 2 tsp Hungarian paprika

Directions

- In a pan, heat the oil on medium heat and sauté the onion and garlic till tender.
- Add the remaining ingredients except the beans and bring everything to a boil.
- Reduce the heat and simmer for about 30 minutes.
- Stir in the beans and cook for 7 minutes.

Amount per serving: 8

Timing Information:

Preparation	15 mins
Total Time	45 mins

Nutritional Information:

Calories	223.9
Fat	5.8g
Cholesterol	0.0mg
Sodium	51.9mg
Carbohydrates	33.5g
Protein	11.2g

* Percent Daily Values are based on a 2,000 calorie diet.

MEDITERRANEAN TOMATO SAUCE

Ingredients

- 2 C. black olives, rinsed
- 2 tbsp olive oil
- 4 -5 cloves garlic, peeled and chopped
- 2 tsp crushed fennel seeds
- 2 C. chopped fresh tomatoes
- 4 -6 minced sun-dried tomatoes (not oil-packed)
- 2 tbsp chopped fresh oregano
- 1/4 C. red wine
- 1/4 C. chopped fresh parsley

Directions

- In a nonreactive skillet, heat the oil on medium heat and sauté the garlic and garlic till for about 1 minute.
- Stir in the remaining ingredients except the parsley and reduce the heat to low.
- Simmer, covered for about 10 minutes.
- Remove everything from the heat and immediately, stir in the parsley.
- Serve warm.

Amount per serving: 1

Timing Information:

Preparation	5 mins
Total Time	15 mins

Nutritional Information:

Calories	189.2
Fat	17.5g
Cholesterol	0.0mg
Sodium	1095.7mg
Carbohydrates	9.3g
Protein	2.2g

* Percent Daily Values are based on a 2,000 calorie diet.

THANKS FOR READING! NOW LET'S TRY SOME **SUSHI** AND **DUMP DINNERS**....

http://bit.ly/2443TFg

To grab this **box set** simply follow the link mentioned above, or tap the book cover.

This will take you to a page where you can simply enter your email address and a PDF version of the **box set** will be emailed to you.

I hope you are ready for some serious cooking!

http://bit.ly/2443TFg

You will also receive updates about all my new books when they are free.

Also don't forget to like and subscribe on the social networks. I love meeting my readers. Links to all my profiles are below so please click and connect :)

Facebook

Twitter

COME ON...
LET'S BE FRIENDS :)

I adore my readers and love connecting with them socially. Please follow the links below so we can connect on Facebook, Twitter, and Google+.

Facebook

Twitter

I also have a blog that I regularly update for my readers so check it out below.

My Blog

CAN I ASK A FAVOUR?

If you found this book interesting, or have otherwise found any benefit in it. Then may I ask that you post a review of it on Amazon? Nothing excites me more than new reviews, especially reviews which suggest new topics for writing. I do read all reviews and I always factor feedback into my newer works.

So if you are willing to take ten minutes to write what you sincerely thought about this book then please visit our Amazon page and post your opinions.

Again thank you!

INTERESTED IN OTHER EASY COOKBOOKS?

Everything is easy! Check out my Amazon Author page for more great cookbooks:

For a complete listing of all my books please see my author page.

Made in the USA
Middletown, DE
28 February 2017